מַעֲרִיב עֲרָבִים/ יוֹצֵר אוֹר

מַעֲרִיב עֲרָבִים

What's your favorite part of the day—morning or evening? Maybe you love the evening! The sun turns from yellow to red, the clouds turn pink, and a beautiful, deep blue-purple spreads across the sky. You can see the first stars start to twinkle as night moves in, and there's a feeling of calm and peace, as if the whole world were settling down to rest. The מַעֲרִיב עֲרָבִים prayer is said every day as daylight turns to evening. It praises God for creating the twilight and the darkness—every single day.

Practice reading these lines from מַעֲרִיב עֲרָבִים.

1. בָּרוּךְ אַתָּה, יְיָ אֱלֹהֵינוּ, מֶלֶךְ הָעוֹלָם,
אֲשֶׁר בִּדְבָרוֹ מַעֲרִיב עֲרָבִים.

2. אֵל חַי וְקַיָּם, תָּמִיד יִמְלֹךְ עָלֵינוּ, לְעוֹלָם וָעֶד.
בָּרוּךְ אַתָּה, יְיָ, הַמַּעֲרִיב עֲרָבִים.

Praised are You, Adonai our God, Ruler of the world, whose word brings on the evening.

May the living and eternal God rule over us always. Praised are You, Adonai, who brings on the evening.

מַעֲרִיב עֲרָבִים

brings on the evening

חַי

living, lives

וְקַיָם

and eternal

יִמְלֹךְ

will rule

WORD MATCH

Connect the English words to the matching Hebrew.

living, lives   מַעֲרִיב עֲרָבִים

will rule   חַי

brings on the evening   וְקַיָם

and eternal   יִמְלֹךְ

COMPLETE THE PHRASE

Fill in the missing word.

מַעֲרִיב _____

brings on the _____

SING ALONG!

Do you know this song?

דָוִד מֶלֶךְ יִשְׂרָאֵל חַי וְקַיָם.

Circle the words in the song that also appear in the מַעֲרִיב עֲרָבִים prayer.

IN THE SYNAGOGUE

מַעֲרִיב עֲרָבִים is said before the *evening* Shema prayer; it has a "partner prayer" that is said before the *morning* Shema. You will learn about the partner prayer—יוֹצֵר אוֹר—in the second part of this chapter, and you will learn about the Shema itself in the next chapter.

יוֹצֵר אוֹר and מַעֲרִיב עֲרָבִים are linked because they remind us that God creates both morning and night, light and darkness. And we praise God for bringing us morning after night after morning . . . day after day after day.

Why do you think we need to say a prayer praising God's creations both in the evening and in the morning?

READING PRACTICE

Practice reading the words below. Watch for the differences between **ע** and **צ**!

. . . .

1. עֶרֶב   מִצְוָה   עִבְרִית   מַצָּה   מַעֲרִיב   צִיצִית

. . . .

2. צַדִּיק   הָעֵץ   צְדָקָה   הַמּוֹצִיא   עֲבוֹדָה   עֲרָבִים

. . . .

ROOTS

Two words in מַעֲרִיב עֲרָבִים look and sound similar.

עֲרָבִים   מַעֲרִיב

> Most Hebrew words are built on roots.
> A root usually consists of three letters.
>
> The two words above share the root ערב.
> ערב means "evening."
>
> Write the root. _____ _____ _____
>
> What does the root ערב mean? _____

Circle the two words with the root ערב—"evening"—in each sentence below.

1. בָּרוּךְ אַתָּה, יְיָ אֱלֹהֵינוּ, מֶלֶךְ הָעוֹלָם, אֲשֶׁר בִּדְבָרוֹ
מַעֲרִיב עֲרָבִים . . .

2. בָּרוּךְ אַתָּה, יְיָ, הַמַּעֲרִיב עֲרָבִים.

Think About This!

Why do you think the prayer begins *and* ends with the statement that God brings on the evening—מַעֲרִיב עֲרָבִים?

יוֹצֵר אוֹר

Maybe you love the daytime. One of the best things about the morning is that it means a new chance to have fun, to learn, and to do something special. Maybe there's a new kid at school you've been waiting to meet, or a soccer match after school. The יוֹצֵר אוֹר prayer is said every morning to praise God for creating the morning light, for giving us renewed energy, and for bringing us the blessing of another day to do good things.

Practice reading these lines from יוֹצֵר אוֹר.

1. בָּרוּךְ אַתָּה, יְיָ אֱלֹהֵינוּ, מֶלֶךְ הָעוֹלָם, יוֹצֵר אוֹר וּבוֹרֵא חֹשֶׁךְ, עֹשֶׂה שָׁלוֹם וּבוֹרֵא אֶת הַכֹּל.

2. בָּרוּךְ אַתָּה, יְיָ, יוֹצֵר הַמְּאוֹרוֹת.

Praised are You, Adonai our God, Ruler of the world, who forms light and creates darkness, who makes peace and creates all things.

Praised are You, Adonai, who forms the lights.

Hebrew	English
יוֹצֵר	forms
אוֹר	light
וּבוֹרֵא	and creates
חֹשֶׁךְ	darkness
עֹשֶׂה	makes
שָׁלוֹם	peace
הַכֹּל	all things, everything

PHRASE MATCH

Connect each Hebrew phrase to the matching English.

and creates all things	יוֹצֵר אוֹר
makes peace	וּבוֹרֵא חֹשֶׁךְ
forms light	עֹשֶׂה שָׁלוֹם
and creates darkness	וּבוֹרֵא אֶת הַכֹּל

WHAT'S MISSING?

Fill in the missing Hebrew word in each phrase.

1. וּבוֹרֵא _____
   and creates *darkness*

2. _____ אֶת הַכֹּל
   and creates all things

3. יוֹצֵר _____
   forms *light*

4. עֹשֶׂה _____
   makes *peace*

CREATION CONTINUES

Both אוֹר יוֹצֵר and מַעֲרִיב עֲרָבִים praise God, the Creator, and describe some of the things that God creates.

This is what אוֹר יוֹצֵר and מַעֲרִיב עֲרָבִים say God does:

1. מַעֲרִיב עֲרָבִים
   brings on the evening

2. יוֹצֵר אוֹר
   forms light

3. בּוֹרֵא חֹשֶׁךְ
   creates darkness

4. עֹשֶׂה שָׁלוֹם
   makes peace

5. בּוֹרֵא אֶת הַכֹּל
   creates all things

Why do you think the prayers include so many words that mean "create"? What does that tell us about God?

_____

_____

_____

A DOUBLE-DUTY DOT

Sometimes the dot for שׁ (shin) and שׂ (sin) identifies the letter *and* the vowel "וֹ".

Read each word below.

קָדֹשׁ וַיַּחֲשֹׁף מֹשֶׁה שָׁלֹשׁ חֹשֶׁךְ

IN THE SYNAGOGUE

There are *two* blessings before the Shema prayer, which you will learn about in the next chapter. Each blessing has an *evening* and a *morning* version. You have already learned the first blessing before the Shema.

First blessing before the Shema

This blessing celebrates the wonder of creation and its renewal each day.

Evening blessing: מַעֲרִיב עֲרָבִים

Morning blessing: יוֹצֵר אוֹר

We also say a second blessing before the Shema.

Second blessing before the Shema

This blessing thanks God for giving us the Torah and mitzvot and—in this way—for showing us love.

Evening blessing: אַהֲבַת עוֹלָם

Morning blessing: אַהֲבָה רַבָּה

After the Shema comes the Ve'ahavta prayer—when we declare *our* love for *God*!

Think About This!

Why do you think we need to declare *our* love for God after describing God's love for *us*?

DRAW THE TIME

Draw a moon and stars above the name of the creation blessing we say at night.

Draw a sun above the name of the creation blessing we say in the morning.

מַעֲרִיב עֲרָבִים   יוֹצֵר אוֹר